# School

Ruth Thomson

Watts Books
London • New York • Sydney

# Note for parents and teachers

The Changing Times series is soundly based on the requirements of the History Curriculum. Using the device of four generations of a real family, the author combines reminiscences of this family with other people's oral evidence. The oral history is matched with photographs and other contemporary sources. Many other lessons are hidden in the text, which practises the skills of chronological sequencing, gives reference to a timeline and introduces the language and vocabulary of the past. Young children will find much useful information here, as well as a new understanding of the recent history of everyday situations and familiar things.

© 1994 Watts Books

Watts Books
96 Leonard Street
London
EC2A 4RH

Franklin Watts Australia
14 Mars Road
Lane Cove
NSW 2066

UK ISBN: 0 7496 1488 9

Dewey Decimal Classification Number 371

10 9 8 7 6 5 4 3 2 1

A CIP catalogue record for this book is available from the British Library.

Editor: Sarah Ridley
Designer: Michael Leaman
Photographer: Peter Millard
Picture researcher: Sarah Moule

The author and publisher would like to thank the following people for their help in the preparation of this book: Debbie, Emma, Andrew, Ron, Gwen and Tom Hallam, Fiona Dodwell, Malcolm Leeke, Suzanne Toleman and children from Market Deeping County Primary School.

Printed in Malaysia

# Contents

This is my school.
It is in our town.
Mum drives me here
every day.

There are 24 children
in my class.
The girls wear
grey tunics or skirts.
The boys wear grey trousers.
Our sweatshirts have the name of the school on them.

We do maths every day.

We practise
making shapes.

We learn about money.

We do maths games
on the computer.

We use calculators
to work out big sums.

We can choose our own reading books.
We take them home at night,
so our mums and dads
can listen to us.

We practise
joined-up writing
in our workbooks.

We are learning
about the Earth.
We find out
about rocks.

Our teacher has read us a story about monsters.

We paint pictures
and make models
of them.

There is a pond
in the school grounds.
In springtime, we dip nets
and jam jars into the water
to see what lives there.

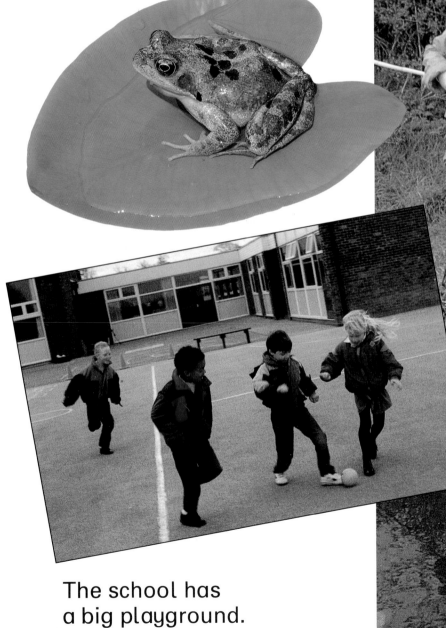

The school has
a big playground.
We play tag and football.

We can skip, catch ball or play chess.

We do gym and
dancing in the hall.

Once a week,
we go swimming.

I asked Dad whether school was the same
when he was young.

He said,

'I went to the village school.
It was so near, I could walk there
by myself.
A lollipop man stood outside
to see us safely across the road.'

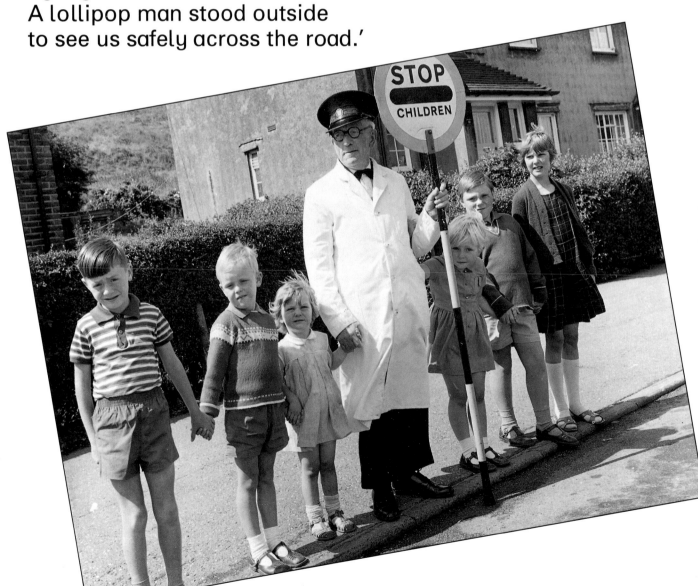

'We sat in pairs at desks with lids that lifted up. The desks were in rows facing the teacher.'

'We learned to read with Janet and John books.'

'There was a pretend shop in the classroom.
We learned a lot of maths by buying, weighing and selling things there.'

I asked Dad about other lessons.

He said,

'We did gym in the hall.
We wore shorts
and vests.'

'A lady came to teach us crafts.
We made raffia mats,
calendars and pots out of clay.'

'Once a week, we listened
to music on the radio.
A presenter told us what to do.
We had to pretend to be trees
or fierce animals.'

'In my last year, a swimming pool
was built in the playground.
I learnt to swim in it.'

County of Lincoln = Parts of Kesteven
Education Committee

First Proficiency
Swimming Certificate

1. Dive from the Side *Sitting* fair standard
2. First Stroke *Breast Stroke* good standard
3. Second Stroke *Back Crawl* fair standard

Awarded to

*Andrew Hallam* School
*Branston C.E. Controlled Primary*
in the 1968 Swimming Season
*A.S. Kemp*
Head Teacher

*E.W.P. Jolley*
Director of Education

PURLEY POOLS

SWIMMING CERTIFICATE

AWARDED TO *Andrew Hallam.* AGE

OF THE *Branston CE Controlled* SCHOOL

WHO CAN NOW SWIM *1 Length (11 yds)* OF THE SCHOOL POOL
*crawl*

*A.S. Kemp* HEADMASTER

*21st June 1968* *M. A. Smith* TEACHER

I asked Dad about playtime and special days.

He said,

'The boys played football
or raced cars downhill.
In the autumn we played
conkers.'

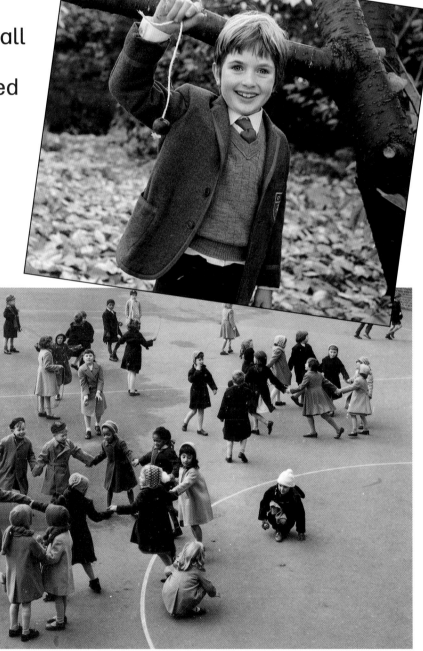

'The girls skipped, played games
and threw balls against the wall.'

14

'On May Day, we put up a maypole
in the playground and danced round it.'

'Once a year, there was a school fete.
Everyone came in fancy dress.
I went as an England footballer,
the year that England won
the World Cup.'

'When Man landed on the Moon,
the whole school watched it on TV.
The headmaster told us
it was an important day in history.'

I asked Grandad about his school days.

He said,

'I went to the same school
as your dad.
There were only four classes
and the toilets were outside.'

'I started school when the Second World War
between England and Germany broke out.'

'We were all given gas masks
in case there was a gas attack.
We practised wearing them,
but we never needed them
for real.'

'Children were sent from big towns to live in our village.
They came to our school.
They told us that their schools had been closed
in case of bombs.'

LEAVE THIS TO US SONNY— **YOU** OUGHT TO BE OUT OF LONDON

MINISTRY OF HEALTH EVACUATION SCHEME

Reading book

I asked Grandad about his lessons.

He said,

'We mostly learned
the three Rs — reading,
writing and arithmetic.'

Maths book

'We also learned
geography and history.'

'We didn't do gym or PE.
We did stretching exercises,
called drill, outside.'

'The school had a garden.
We helped to grow vegetables.
There was a shortage of food
because of the war.'

2000                                               1975                                      1950

I asked Grandad what he remembers most
about his school days.

He said,

'The best lessons were nature walks.
Sometimes, we went down to the stream
and caught sticklebacks.
We put them in an aquarium
on the windowsill.'

'There were two playgrounds —
one for boys and one for girls.
We spent a lot of time playing marbles.'

'At playtime, we had
little bottles of milk
with cardboard tops.
In winter,
the milk froze.'

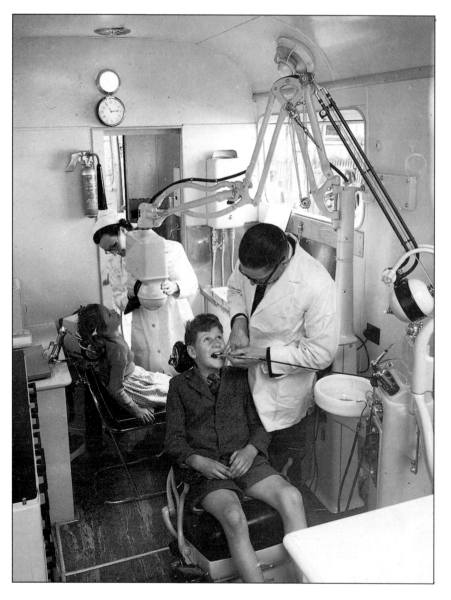

'Once a year, a caravan appeared
in the playground.
It was the dentist.
One time, he pulled two of my teeth out.'

Great-grandad went to the same school
from the age of 5 until he left at the age of 14.

He said,

'We didn't wear a uniform.
Boys wore knickerbockers
and shirts with stiff collars.
Girls wore dresses, often
with a white pinafore on top.'

Stiff collar

'We sat at desks in rows.
We had to sit up straight.
The teacher stood at the front
of the class by the blackboard.'

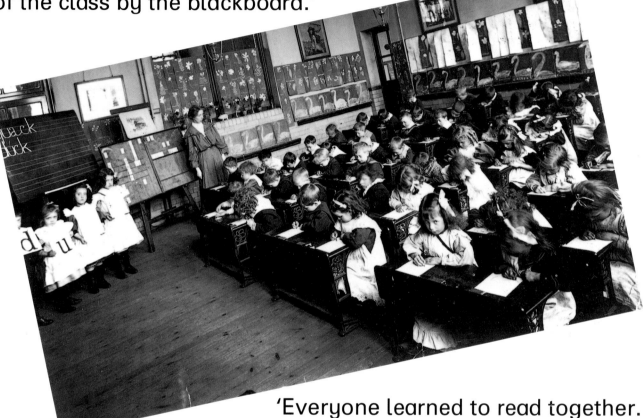

'Everyone learned to read together.
The teacher pointed
to a word on the blackboard
and we all read it out.'

'When we could read,
we took turns to read aloud
a few sentences each
from a reading book.'

23

Great-grandad told me
about learning to write.

He said,

'The youngest children learnt
to draw letters in a tray of sand.
They wrote with a pointed stick.'

'Later, we practised writing
with slate pencils on slates.
They made a horrible squeak.'

Ink

'When we were older,
we wrote with pen and ink.
We had inkwells in our desks.
We dipped the pens into the ink.'

Ink jug for
filling inkwells

Dip pen

Inkwell

*Pitt the Earl of Chatham a famous statesman.*
*Pitt the Earl of Chatham a famous statesman.*
*Pitt the Earl of Chatham a famous statesman.*
*Pitt the Earl of Chatham a famous statesman*
*Pitt the Earl of Chatham a famous statesman.*
*Quebec was captured by General Wolfe in 1759.*
*Quebec was captured by General Wolfe in 1759.*
*Quebec was captured by General Wolfe in 1759.*

*Revolution completed by flight of James II.*

*South Sea Scheme inaugurated by Harley.*
*South Sea Scheme inaugurated by Harley.*

'We wrote in a copy book.
We copied out the printed writing
four times, as neatly as we could.'

I asked Great-grandad
what else he did at school.

He said,

'We learned about kings and queens
and other countries.'

Globe

'We went on nature walks
and painted flowers and insects.'

'We had
drawing lessons.
Sometimes,
we copied patterns
on drawing cards.'

Skipping rope

Marbles

Whip and top

Five stones

'At playtime, we played marbles or five stones. The girls skipped or played with hoops or whips and tops.'

Hoop

SCS
LEAGUE
CHAMPIONS
1919.

'When I was old enough, I played in my school football team.'

I asked Great-grandad what he remembers
most about school.

He said,

'The teachers were very strict.
If you misbehaved, you were sent
to the headmaster.
He caned you on the hand.'

'One of the best things was Empire Day.
We dressed up and had a parade
through the village.'

'At the end of the year, there was a prize-giving.'

'Children got certificates for good work.'

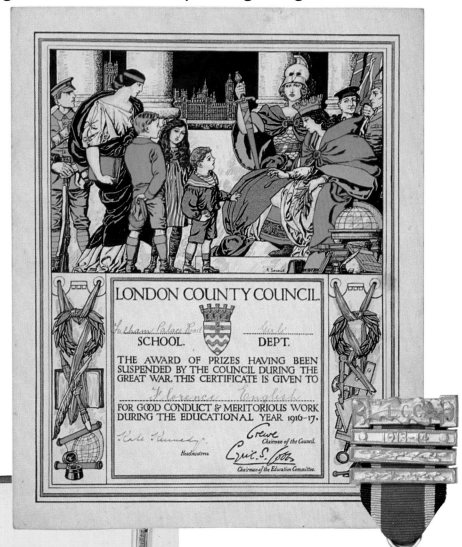

LONDON COUNTY COUNCIL.

*Fulham Palace Road* SCHOOL. *Girls'* DEP'T.

THE AWARD OF PRIZES HAVING BEEN SUSPENDED BY THE COUNCIL DURING THE GREAT WAR, THIS CERTIFICATE IS GIVEN TO

*Florence English*

FOR GOOD CONDUCT & MERITORIOUS WORK DURING THE EDUCATIONAL YEAR 1916-17.

*Kate Kennedy.*
Headmistress

*Crewe*
Chairman of the Council.

*Eric S. Cobb*
Chairman of the Education Committee.

'Sometimes, we were given books as prizes.'

LONDON COUNTY COUNCIL

*All Saints' School* SCHOOL

AWARDED TO

*Edward Fifield*

FOR *Industry, Conduct & Attendance*

*E. L. Davis*
HEAD TEACHER

*July 16th 1915.*

'I was once given a medal for not missing a single day's school all year.'

# Things to do

In Great-grandad's time,
girls and boys had some lessons separately.
Girls learnt to cook, wash laundry and sew.
Boys had woodwork lessons.

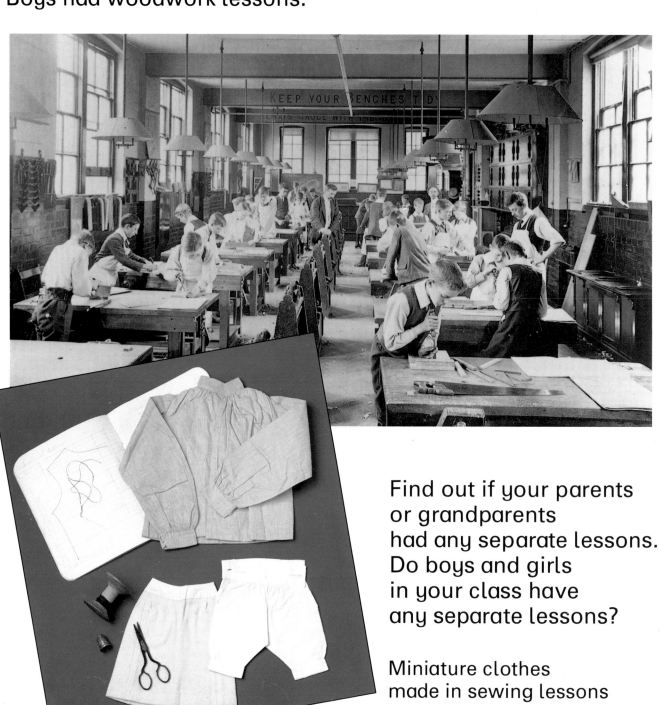

Find out if your parents
or grandparents
had any separate lessons.
Do boys and girls
in your class have
any separate lessons?

Miniature clothes
made in sewing lessons

Dumb-bells

Show these pictures to different grown-ups.
Find out if they used any of these objects at school.
What were the objects used for?

Clock face

Indian clubs

Abacus

Pencil box

Pastry tools

# Index

Photographs: Barnabys Picture Library front cover tl, 22b; Cambridge and County Folk Museum 16bl; Camera Press 12bl; Bruce Coleman Ltd 8tl; Collections 11tr; Chris Fairclough 9b; Greater London Record Office endpapers, title page b, 13t, 23t, 30t; Jill Gray Collection/Peter Millard front cover bl, imprint page, 11c, 12t, 12br, 18t, 18b, 21bl, 23b, 24t, 24bl, 25(all), 26(all), 27tl, 27tr, 28t, 29(all), 30b, 31(all); Andrew Hallam 13b, 15bl; Thomas Hallam 27b; Hulton Deutsch Collection Ltd 15t, 16br, 19t, 19b, 20; Robert Harding Picture Library 14t; courtesy of the Trustees of the Imperial War Museum 17b; Peter Millard front cover br, title page t, 4-5, 6-7, 8r, 8bl, 9t, 21tl, 22t; Popperfoto front cover tr, 10, 11br, 18c; Science Photo Library 15br; Mr Stead 16t; Topham Picture Library 14b, 17t, 21br, 24br, 28b.